Mixed Emotions

Mixed Emotions

Devlin Bell

Copyright © 2009 by Devlin Bell.

Library of Congress Control Number: 2009903914
ISBN: Hardcover   978-1-4415-3060-8
               Softcover   978-1-4415-3059-2

All rights reserved. No part of this book may be reproduced or transmitted in any form or by any means, electronic or mechanical, including photocopying, recording, or by any information storage and retrieval system, without permission in writing from the copyright owner.

This book was printed in the United States of America.

To order additional copies of this book, contact:
Xlibris Corporation
1-888-795-4274
www.Xlibris.com
Orders@Xlibris.com
58635

CONTENTS

The Book 9
Mind Free 10
Step step 11
Time 12
Awaking 13
Reflection 14
Not Forgetting Love 15
Truly Beautiful 16
A Rose 17
Tired 18
The Secret To My Heart 19
Caught Up 20
Good To Me 21
Loneliness 22
Love in the Air 23
What Could It Be? 24
Where's the Dressing? 25
Reflections of Lost Love 26
Invisible Bubble 27
Choices 28
How do you say that I love you? 29
Brother Man 30
I'm Thinking About 31
The Tumbling Walls 32
The Doors 34
The Sacred Love 35
Shell of Emptiness 36
Spank That Child 37
The Color Earth 39
The World 40
Who Am I 41

Confusion 42
Cruel Intentions 44
How Do I Defuse the Flames? 45
I am Somebody 46
I See You 48
Let Me Be 50

*To future wife, my family, and true friends.
I would never have the strength and encouragement
to complete this book. Thank you so much!*

The Book

Come and open my book. Read it if you can.
Come and indulge in this precious literature
And find out about this mysterious man.

If you want deep conversation, try chapters 1,2,3.
If you want this book to be good for you,
You must relax and let your mind run free.

If you like excitement, try chapters 4, 7 and 22.
But if you want Love, well the rest of the book will do.

It will play with mental thoughts
And make your body hum.
You wouldn't know what to do
When you're finished or done

It's enchanting.
It will be hard to put it down once you begin.
The pages will overwhelm you.
You will enjoy telling your closest friend.

If you would like to read this book, it's free
And this is what you must do.
Just take a few steps forward and say
"Hi, how are you?"

Mind Free

My mind is not whole
My body is not free.
My body is warm, but I'm still lonely.
I throw up a wall because I still feel pain.
Don't ask me what it is because I can't explain.
I quiver and shake, at night dreaming to have someone
To hold and kiss.
For that is the affection that I truly miss.
I have friends that I can call on the phone.
But still in my heart and mind
I'm all alone.

Step step

Step into my mind, of my thoughts of you
Step into my feelings, what I feel is true.
Visualize what you have by closing your eyes.
Is it there, is it there, is it there.
One must release, before it is given.
But, I don't know how. I don't know how.
One must release, before it is given.
Allow me to show you the way.
Step into my heart, of my feelings for you.
Step into my thoughts, what I think is true.
Embrace my hand.
How do you feel?
Am I telling you a lie, or are my feelings real.
To build a wall it takes one brick at a time.
To knock it down, one blast would do fine.
One must release before it is given.
Step into my mind, of my thoughts of you.
Step into my heart. For what I feel is true.

Time

Time, a four letter word that means so much.
The power of a second.
What would happen, if I could take it back.
If it was given.
What if you don't have it.
Time in a relationship
But what I think, does it matter.
It matters if you have it or you don't.
Time oh my, oh my.
Where have you gone?
Come, come back to me.
If only I could go back in time.
I would change the way.
To bring time back to us.
So we can be together.

Awaking

Awaking is the setting of the moon.
I'm dying.
I'm leaving going to leave my family soon.
There is a mystical aroma; I wonder what it could be.
It's an awful feeling, and it's choking me.
It's trying to steal my breath, and then slice away my heart.
The force is extremely strong,
and it won't stop until it tears me apart.
I tried to hide in shelter,
and hope that it wouldn't find me there.
I tried to tell someone else, but they wouldn't listen.
They just stare
There is a feeling of rebellion, maybe I don't want to stop.
Maybe I can transform to a bunny, and hop, hop, hop
Can I run from a bullet, maybe I can dodge it
It might miss me.
Oh here it comes again my heart is beating so fast, slow down.
Stop, stop, and stop.
My stomach is hurting; it feels like it's in knots.
My body is losing its heat.
My eyes are losing its sight.
I was caught, my running was in vein.
If I would have stood still.
The consequences would have been the same.
As the lights goes dim.
Wow, I can only wish.
For the things I can change.
I know everything I want to do right now.
It's only me to blame.
Even tho I'm about to go to sleep.
I'm awake!!!!

Reflection

Like a reflection from a mirror; a mirror shines
I wish you were in my arms I wish you were mine
Me being next to you.
Put my heart in a flame.
I know it's all my fault only me to blame.
But once in your life you must take a chance.
That's the only way to find true romance.
I want you, can you feel the wind
But before we become lovers we must become friends.
Love is nothing without friendship
Friendship is nothing without caring.
I care for you do you care for me.
That is I must know before we begin to fly.
Otherwise we can just shake hands,
And go our separate ways without saying goodbye.
A friend.
Emotions running wild in which way should I go I don't know.
The gray man says give up, you're better off dead.
My heart were born,
I was there to see.
But after a few years they
Emotions running wild

Not Forgetting Love

There's no light switch in love
Turning it on or off.

There's not a heart that can catch a cold and began to cough
Once feelings start, they can never disappear.

But in our case, our love will always be here.
My love for you is like a fiery flame.

You can throw cold water on me and
I will still be the same.

Your not being here is like soup without a spoon
I wish I could be with you soon.

Believe me, you will never be forgotten
There will always be a place for you here in my heart.

Not Forgetting Love.

Truly Beautiful

In a mind stance I see you in a distance
appealing to everyone, especially to me.
Your eyes wondering then finally we connect.
What a beautiful sight to see.

I move forward and so do you
I await your embrace
Truly Beautiful

When I feel you, my body yearns wanting you.
In my mind I know you are the one.
Truly Beautiful

The words you speak is a reflection of spring in the air.
Your aroma is an attraction by itself.
Truly Beautiful

I am so amazed. I feel you wanting me. Is it True?
Because I want you to know beautiful one that I want you too.
Truly Beautiful

A Rose

The wind may blow from East to West
When it rains, it rains hard.

A flower may bloom in the spring
Not just any flower but a Rose.

A flower so beautiful and smell so delightful
I could only compare to you.

A King of its kind and so are you, a Queen to my eyes
Never have I seen such beauty.

In the spring before it blooms, the rose is closed.

But with time the flowers will bloom
And so will our friendship

I could only compare your beauty to such a flower

A Rose

Tired

I'm tired of these things that people say
Most times they don't know anything anyway.

Just talking, talking, talking, don't know what it's about.
I wish that person would shut up their mouth.
Just look, they're saying things that hurt people lives.
They don't care, they don't even think twice.

They just make up things, they just lie.
I wish someone would get fed up and poke them in the eye.

What I'm trying to say is Keep Your Mouth Shut.
Stop Talking All That Dirt.

Before you will be that big mouth sucker that gets hurt.

The Secret To My Heart

Somewhere in my travels, seeking, trying to find
That loveliness that's called the secret to my life.
Far, yet wide I looked, but stumbled on a few that gave me hope.
In the mist of things, I wanted to stop.
But the winds shoot up and blew me to the East.
I was knocked down on my back with my eyes closed.
When I looked up, you were there.
Bright eyes, pretty smile, a humble heart.
Like a ray of sunshine, you warmed my heart.
Brought happiness to me.
The Secret To My Heart

Caught Up

Caught up in a process of misunderstanding
Belief in the believer, to whom do you believe?
Trust your life in another's hands,
Will you stay or leave?
Why? Why? Why? We all ask ourselves.
Why am I here? Is there a purpose for my life?
Most of us don't know the answer
But we choose not to listen.
Dodging the trust and embracing the lie.
Are you truly happy?
What will make you happy?
Decisions are made every day,
Every hour, every minute.
What do you decide?
Actions speak louder than words.
What do your actions say?
If you don't know, then you're caught up.

Good To Me

Why am I so blind that I can't see?
That everything I want is given to me.
I have courage that you gave me your word.
I have faith that my voice will be heard.
I have knowledge when I read I will know.
I have a strong body that can take me
Anywhere I want to go.
Why is it so blind that I can't see?
That I've been blessed already
And you've been good to me.

Loneliness

"Loneliness seems like a friend", well that's
what he told me when she moved in.

Sometimes my heart feels like an empty shell
nothing in it and began to swell.

Being with no one is a scary fright
I hope someone can fix this sight.

Loneliness that's a powerful word
I wish it was something I never heard.

Yes indeed, it happened to me.
Every time I look at my reflection I can see.

What do I see, a lonely man
without worth and love in his hands.

What will I do, just wonder about
until this thing called loneliness
moves its way out.

Love in the Air

Peace of mind,
Beautiful like a willow tree in the fall.
A cool breeze on a hot summer's day.
Love is in the air.

A hot shower to relax your body.
A good meal to start your day.
The sound of birds dropping in the wind.
Love is in the air.

Oh My, here I am standing.
With my hands raised up in the wind.
Stacked down to the ground.
Speaking to the wind, asking, pleading.
So that one day it could be deflected to me.
Love is in the air.

What Could It Be?

I feel you next to me, what could it be?

Thoughts are surrounding my mind
Colors are flashing in my head.

Missing and wanting you, what could it be?

Talking to you makes me feel a high.
Embracing you makes me feel loved.

Being and speaking to you, what could it be?

Kissing your soft lips.
Looking into your eyes.

Touching and want you, what could it be?

I feel you next to me, what could it be?

It's you. It's my Destiny!!!

Where's the Dressing?

Everything looks good, the time is right.
The table is set, here comes the candlelight.
The smell is delightful, my body is starting to shake.
My mouth is watering, awaiting my plate.
But where's the dressing?

I'll have a little leg of this and maybe a little of that.
The buns are still hot and my stomach is in a knot.
But where's the dressing?

The wine is fine, but I'm about to lose my mind.
Where is the dressing?

Everything is so neat but my meal is not complete.
The dressing is the highlight of my meal.
Without that, the meal is not big deal.
Where is the dressing?

I can't make the dressing myself.
Maybe I'll look somewhere else.
I'm not hard to satisfy.
I need my dressing to stay alive.
Where is the dressing?

Reflections of Lost Love

My pulse is beating slowly.
My face has lost its lift.
My will has forgotten how to fight.
I'm glaring at nothing but space.
Reflections of lost love.

Feelings of loneliness, un-wantedness,
Internal pain
One would say my body was soulless.
I want my body to be warm again.
Reflections of lost love.

Embracing the wind, holding a pillow.
Wanting to be touched.
The exchange of one voice to another.
I only wonder if, but when the night falls
I have no one to love.
Reflections of lost love.

Invisible Bubble

I See You, I See You,
But you don't have a clue.
I'm trapped in an invisible bubble.
I can't break out. I can't get through.
My thoughts surround your every move.
And every breath that you take.
But I'm still trapped in this bubble that I don't know how to break.
I feel as if I'm hurting you. I'm losing my mind.
Hopefully this bubble will loosen up or dissolve in time.
The feelings I have for you are not hidden, they are here.
I don't know what this bubble is doing.
I hope it disappears.

Choices

Words of expression pay tribute to a heart of lies.
Confusion of an empty mess is a bitterness of pleasure,
Dipped in a pot of blindness.
One can't see, but needs to be guided.
Being locked in a room with a bang.
One loses their ears and can't hear a thing.
But still struggling, struggling to find a way.
A way. A way to what? The hell if I know.
But I do, but I don't want to, but still,
I don't know how. Words are of great power.
If they emerge inside, they can be
beneficial or deadly to your mind.
Ways of direction is yours.
The ways of direction is a choice you make.
Listen or not. It's up to you.
See or choose to be blind.
I must live, you must live,
With the answer of your choice.
Is it? Is it? Is it?
Is it words of expression?
Or is it words of lies?
It's your choice. You make it.

How do you say that I love you?

A Move, A Gesture, A Note, A Smile,
How do you say that I love you?
A Gift. A Touch.
How do you say that I love you?
There are many ways of showing love.
Some are better than others.
Expression, the look in your eyes.
The plans that you made for the future to come.
How do you say that I love you?
You don't.
You show it.
That's how you know I love you.

Brother Man

My Brother Man,
Why are you going to lift that by yourself?

Why don't you ask for help?
and ask someone else.

My Brother Man
Are you going to that place alone?

Why don't you ask someone to go with you?
Call them on the phone.

Why is it that you have so much pride?
If you don't watch it, it will eat you alive.

Hey My Brother Man!!!
What's up with you?

Why do you do the things that you do?
There are others on this land, that are just like you.

I'm Thinking About

I'm sitting here thinking about how I wish it will be,
Holding you in my hands, Embracing you in my arms,
Yes that sounds good to me.

I'm thinking about how time was spent,
I don't think I wasted a dime.
Because I shared every moment with you . . . and yes . . .
Every moment was sweet and divine.

I'm thinking about when I visualize in my mind,
It gives my heart a jump start,
And make me feel good every time.

When I think about kissing you,
I enjoy your lips and I enjoy your taste.

Conversation with you puts my body in a trance.
Making me want you more.

What I'm really thinking
is . . .
I want you right now.

The Tumbling Walls

These old walls are tumbling down,
And I'm beginning a fresh new start.

I have faithful teachers who
Equip me with a soft-like heart.

I'm always thanking them,
Because without them where will I be?

Now I have a vision for God,
How I can see.

I had to crawl before I could walk.

I had to listen before I could talk.

But I know the time is here.

I must use what I have learned,
And not be afraid to be burned.

Because now the lord is looking out for me,
Even more than the devil may be lurking.

I'll never stop waiting.

I'm going to give it my all,
Going to give it the best that I can.

Now I'm no longer known as worldly,

But a **Christian**

The Doors

The opening of doors, to a new horizon.
Adventure to the adventurous.
What is to be expected?
What is wanted?
Is it wanted? What do you want?
Each minute brings me closer.
But still should I open it?
Or should I stay away?
One would say. If you feel heat from a door, don't open it.
But, what kind of heat do I feel.
Is it the heat of love?
Exciting, but yet could it satisfy.
Satisfy your hunger, for time, respect, your hunger for love.
Each moment makes me want you.
My body is on the floor, but my mind is on hold.
The point is getting to know.
I want to get to know you better.
To a new horizon,
What is to be expected?
Is it wanted?
Is it?
What is it that you want?
OPEN THE DOORS.

The Sacred Love

You can be my lover or friend
For that's the kind of love that sticks to the end.
When I spend time with you, strange feelings comes and goes.
Feelings of crying, sharing a tear, laughter and passion in which you must know.
My mind says one thing but my body says another.
Sometimes I get confused and wonder if I want you for more than a friend or just a lover.
Many days and nights go by. I wonder what you're doing or who's sleeping by your side.
Like a river flow, you hurt till I bleed.
Because you're two things that's dear to me and all that I need.

Shell of Emptiness

Dwindling dimensions hanging on a seam.
Sparkles in low places what does all this mean?
Creation is in a mist of misunderstanding.
How did we get here? Most of us don't know.
I'm peddling, trying to go upstream.
The river was rough but now it's dry.
In order to reach the goal,
No longer can we live like we do. We must die.
Emotions rebelling, causing one to fight against another.
Slowly eating the insides of your soul within.
It will become an empty shell.
A worker for not him but him, living in a bubble of confusion.
It is up to them, the sunshine of hope
To pierce the bubble and fill the empty shell.
Turning confusion into understanding.
Understanding into knowledge.
Taking them under their wing.
Soon they will fly and rescue someone else.

Spank That Child

If the child won't sit in the seat, and starts to kick their feet.
Spank That Child

If the kid is very lazy, but he still acts crazy.
Spank That Child

If the kid refuses to wait, the gives you a headache.
Spank That Child

If the kid refuses to eat, then doesn't go to sleep.
Spank That Child

If the child is in class lurking and not working.
Spank That Child

If you tell your child to "Come here Hun", but they start to run.
Spank That Child

If the child is rude, then starts to throw their food.
Spank That Child

Spank That Child Spank That Child Spank That Child

For some reason, parents are afraid to reach out and touch.

Like they said, "Spare the rod, Spoil the child."

Back in the day, the teacher whipped me, the principal whipped me.
Mama then Papa.

Spank That Child Spank That Child

If the kid is running the streets, the kid should feel the heat.
Spank That Child

If the kid wants to act up, you should tap that butt.
Spank That Child

When kids don't want to act right, and he wants to fight.
Spank That Child

If the kid acts up in the store, then fall out on the floor.
Spank That Child

The Color Earth

The Earth is bowl of different colors.
Red, Yellow, Orange, and Green.

So why should there be one color
to me it seem.

What is this thing called
a dominant race.

I think all the other colors should
step up and put them in their place
but NO!!
someone should talk to them
and make them understand.

That the Earth won't be as beautiful
with one color covering the land.

The World

What have I ever done?
The price I had to pay.
Because their different from me.
Are they afraid?
I say oh yeah.
Of me...
And
The rest of the world

Who Am I
???

Who am I? A thing without a soul
Who am I? A thing that still grows old
Who am I? A thing that stuck in its fears
Who am I? A thing that shed tears
Loving but no love, caring but thoughtless
Giving but keep to self
Knowledgeable but hold it all in
Not letting anyone in his life
Who am I?
I will tell you what I'm not
A Christian!

Confusion

My emotional feelings are direct but indirect
but serves no purpose.
In which way should I go?
I don't know what's the use of having a full glass of beverage
And cannot drink.
Why try to use your mind,
When it's cluttered with nonsense and can't even think.
What is the beauty of the rose
If you can't take a deep breath and smell.
Why should I take a chance if I already know in my mind
That I'm going to fail.
I'm looking at a picture.
When I look deeply,
I see all the things that I want to find.
But when others look at this picture,
They get a different perspective in their minds.
They see but they can't believe it.
They want to believe something else.
That's why most times it's best for me to keep to myself.
All things are not wonderful. If you get tossed up,
You will never know where you will land.
But when I put up a wall,
You will never have a chance to advance.
All these feelings of emptiness separates me,
Shattering my heart.
Like a fish bowl with no fish.
Empty, but meaningless.
Where do I start?
Maybe if I stand still, then take a step back

I will notice what it is and find out where it's at.

Cruel Intentions

I walk searching, awaiting to find,
The wonderful feeling to have something that's mine.
To be and have peace within. But most times I don't fit in.
To have something you want, but something you're not.
Something beautiful to you, but yourself is not beautiful.
I'm walking and my surrounding starts to change.
Most of the things I know still remain.
To be needed, to be wanted, to be special, to be loved.
My intentions are plain, but are so, so difficult to have at hand.
So what I have to do is change, change into that other man.
Oh my that's cruel.
Cruel Intentions.

To be changed for a change.
To have a change that needed to be changed.
To have what you want, but is that what you want?
Why is it so cruel to be a paint brush for someone else,
to be with someone else?
But the cruel effect is the true effect.
Of what needed to be changed.
To achieve the highest achievement any man wants to have.
To have something you want to love.
But especially, have it love you back.
Something you want, have it love you back.
But it's not here.
Not there at all
Cruel Intentions.

How Do I Defuse the Flames?

I can't understand what you have done to me.
I can't get you out of my mind.
Some would say months, weeks, maybe days.
I feel empty within hours of your last call.
Your sweet loving voice jelled with my heart.
Becoming a necessity to my life.
I tried to push you away.
But the more I do, the more I want you.
I can't understand what you have done to me.
Where I look into your eyes,
I see my spirit dancing with yours.
I see a love from a child for their mother.
I see peace of an eagle flying in the wind.
I see comfort.
When I'm with you, you turn my blood into a fuel.
Every time, I'm with you. I ignite.
The flames burn hard.
I don't know how to defuse the flames.
I don't believe in witchcraft.
But there is an essence that overwhelms my mental thoughts.
Pulling my whole self towards your essence.
Making it extremely hard for me.
When I'm without you. I visualize you constantly.
What am I to do?
How do I defuse the flames?
Maybe I don't want to
I don't understand what you've done to me.

I am Somebody

When I look into the mirror, what do I see?
I see one of GOD's creation staring at me.

I am somebody from head to toe.
I take pride with me everywhere I go.

When I look deeper in the mirror
I see color and texture unlike anyone else.

The only one who can predict my future is myself.
I make my own future, I pave my own way.
But in order to reach those goals I must start today.

There's no river that's too wide,
There's no rope that's too strong,
If only you believe in GOD.

I will get there no matter how long.
There are no limit to what I could do.
There are no goal that I can't achieve.

If only you know that I am somebody.
If only that I can believe.

But before I get up or before I go away,
There are some words that give me strength
And encouragement and something that I want to say:

I am beautiful, I am beautiful
I have beauty within me, I have beauty within me.

The knowledge of GOD is my power.
The knowledge of GOD is my power.

I want that power within me.
I can accomplish any goal that I think of

Because I am Somebody/ I am Somebody

I See You

With a twinkle of an eye
I See You . . . I See You . . .

I see a glow that I want to know.
My mind says, "No"
But my body says, "Hell Yes, Let's Go!"

I See You . . . I See You . . .

I see a smile that I will allow you to dial
the combination to my heart
and unlock the love that I have locked within.

I see my hand reaching out for yours to caress
To bring me closer to your chest
So we can dance with finesse.

Ohhh Yes . . . I See You . . .

I see and I know that you're so fine.
And if you allow me to spend time,
I know that you will be mine.

I See You . . . I See You . . .

When you let me in.
One second seems like one minute.
One minute seems like one hour.
One hour seems like one month.

Oh, I'm sorry, reverse that.
A month seems like an hour.
An hour seems like a minute.
A minute seems like a second.

What I'm saying is I lose time with you.

When I look into your eyes.
I'm so surprised.
And then I realize that you see the same thing too.

I See You . . . I See You . . .

Let Me Be

Let me be the water to cool your thirst.
I want to be your shade from the hot sun.
Let me be your shelter from the rain.
I want to be your blanket to keep you warm from the cold.
Let me be your strength to move things.
Let me be your pillow when you lay down.
Let me be the one you call when you're feeling bad.
Let me be the one you Love.
Let Me Be . . . Let Me Be.